Marvel Studios' *Ant-Man and The Wasp*

Based on the Screenplay by
Chris McKenna, Erik Sommers,
Paul Rudd, Andrew Barrer, and Gabriel Ferrari

Story by
Stan Lee, Larry Lieber,
Jack Kirby, and Ernie Hart

Produced by Kevin Feige, p.g.a.,
and Stephen Broussard
Directed by Peyton Reed

Level 2

Retold by Jane Rollason

Series Editors: Andy Hopkins and Jocelyn Potter

T0345466

Pearson Education Limited
KAO Two
KAO Park, Harlow,
Essex, CM17 9NA, England
and Associated Companies throughout the world.

ISBN: 978-1-2923-4745-5
This edition first published by Pearson Education Ltd 2018
1 3 5 7 9 10 8 6 4 2

The authors have asserted their moral rights in accordance
with the Copyright Designs and Patents Act 1988

Set in 9pt/14pt Xenois Slab Pro
Printed by Neografia, Slovakia

Published by Pearson Education Limited

For a complete list of the titles available in the Pearson English Readers series, visit
www.pearsonenglishreaders.com.
Alternatively, write to your local Pearson Education office or
to Pearson English Readers Marketing Department,
Pearson Education, KAO Two, KAO Park, Harlow, Essex, CM17 9NA

Contents

Who's Who?

Scott Lang / Ant-Man

He stole an Ant-Man suit, and then he had Ant-Man powers. The suit makes the wearer very large or very small. Scott used it when he helped in a fight between some of the Avengers. Now, after the fight, he is under house arrest.

Cassie Lang

She is Scott's ten-year-old daughter. She lives with her mother, but sometimes visits her father. They cannot leave his house on her visits, but he plays wonderful games with her.

Hope van Dyne / The Wasp

She lives and works with her father, Hank Pym. When she wears her Wasp suit, she can shrink to the size of a wasp. She made Scott a better fighter, and taught him the control of her father's helper/giant ants.

Hank Pym and Janet van Dyne

They are scientists, and Hope's parents. Hank made the Ant-Man and The Wasp suits, and he was the first Ant-Man. Now, the FBI* is looking for him. Janet was the first Wasp. She is in the Quantum** Realm and cannot leave.

* FBI: a U.S. agency with offices in every state. FBI agents try to stop dangerous people before they hurt other people or the country.
** quantum: one of the smallest possible parts of things, and of energy

Ava Starr / Ghost

Her quantum scientist father, Elihas Starr, worked with Hank, but it ended badly. When her parents died in a lab accident, the quantum energy hurt Ava. The U.S. agency S.H.I.E.L.D.* taught her to use this power for her country, but she is slowly dying—and very dangerous.

Bill Foster

He is a scientist. He worked with Hank and Elihas. Now, he teaches quantum science. After Elihas died, he was a father to Ava. He helped her control her powers.

Agent Jimmy Woo

He works for the FBI. He watches Scott because Scott can't leave his house. He also wants to catch Hank and Hope. The FBI want them, too, because Scott used their technology in the Avengers' fight.

Luis

He is Scott's best friend. They met in prison. When they left prison, they couldn't find work. Now, the two friends are starting a new technology company.

Sonny Burch

He buys—or steals—technology parts. Then, he sells them. He is only interested in money. He knows an FBI agent, and he pays the agent for his help.

---

* S.H.I.E.L.D.: in this story, a powerful U.S. agency. S.H.I.E.L.D. agents fight other countries, and other worlds.

Introduction

"A tunnel to the Quantum Realm!" cried Hope excitedly. *"Dad, what are you saying ...?"*

"I think we can bring your mother home," Hank said.

Janet van Dyne is in the Quantum Realm, and she cannot leave. In that subatomic world, everything is very small. People can go there from Earth when they shrink to subatomic size in one of Hank's suits.

Hank and Hope want to find Janet, but they don't know her location. Only one person knows—Ant-Man. But there's a problem. Ant-Man is under house arrest and he can't leave home.

After college, Scott Lang worked for VistaCorp, a giant tech company. It stole from its customers, and Scott didn't like that. He stole money from VistaCorp and gave it to the customers. For that, he went to prison for three years. His wife Maggie left him and she married again. But they are Cassie's parents—and they are friends.

After Scott's time in prison, Hank gave him the job of the new Ant-Man. Scott started to fall in love with Hope, and she liked him, too. But then, Captain America wanted Scott to help him in a big fight between some of the Avengers in Germany. The U.S.—and the world—was very unhappy about this fight. Scott didn't say anything to Hank or Hope before he left. But when Ant-Man's suit was giant size, he was on T.V. ...

Marvel Studios' Ant-Man and The Wasp (2018) is the 20th movie in the Marvel Cinematic Universe. It was the second movie about Ant-Man, after *Marvel Studios' Ant-Man* in 2015. Paul Rudd plays Ant-Man and Evangeline Lilly is The Wasp.

Prologue: San Francisco

The missile moved slowly. Its nose turned to San Francisco, and it started to move faster. It was on its way.

An ant and a wasp jumped onto the missile. They weren't really an ant and a wasp. They were Hank Pym and Janet van Dyne, in their Ant-Man and The Wasp suits.

"We have to stop it!" The Wasp shouted.

"We have to get inside!" Ant-Man called to his wife.

But they couldn't get inside. They were very small, but they were too big for *this* job. Hank wanted to go subatomic, but his suit didn't work.

"I'll go," Janet said. "My suit's working."

"But you'll fall into the Quantum Realm," Hank cried. "Then, you can't come back. I'll never see you again."

"I love you and Hope!" Janet shouted. Before Hank could stop her, she shrank to subatomic size. She flew inside the missile, and found the controls. She quickly changed some numbers. The missile fell into the ocean, and Janet fell into the Quantum Realm.

Many years later

"Many people lived that day because of your mother, Hope. But it was the worst day of my life," Hank said sadly. He sat across the table from his daughter. "You were seven years old, and I had to come home without your mother."

Hope's eyes were wet.

"But later, Scott used my Ant-Man suit and went to the Quantum Realm. Then, he *came back!*" Hank said. "His trip changed everything. And now—look!" he said. "I found these old plans."

"A tunnel to the Quantum Realm!" cried Hope excitedly. "Dad, what are you saying ...?"

"I think we can bring your mother home," Hank said.

"Three days? That's easy!"

Today

BRRRRRR!

The noise—inside and outside Scott's house—was very loud. Five minutes later, there were FBI agents in every room. They looked under his bed, in his washing machine, and inside his closet.

"It's my weekend with Cassie, Agent Woo," Scott said. Cassie was Scott's ten-year-old daughter. "We were in the yard. I put *one foot* outside the yard! It was an accident. It was the foot with the tracker. Really, you don't have to do this."

"You know that we *do*, Scott," Agent Woo answered. He sent his number two, Agent Stoltz, upstairs.

"Why are you always here?" Cassie asked.

"I'm sorry, Cassie," Agent Woo said. He smiled and spoke slowly. "Think of it this way. Your school says, 'You can't write on the walls.' So you don't write on the walls. Your dad went to Germany and 'wrote on the walls' with Captain America. That was very bad, and now he's under house arrest for two years. He can't leave this house. He can't use Avenger technology. He can't meet any of the Avengers. He can't talk to Hank Pym or Hope van Dyne. One mistake, and he'll go to prison for twenty years. O.K., Cassie?"

Cassie looked bored.

"*WOW!*" Scott said. "You're really great with children!"

"And one more question for *you*, Scott," Agent Woo said. "Did you meet Hank or Hope last week?"

"No," Scott answered. "I'm not stupid. After two years, I only have three more days of house arrest."

"And Hank and Hope hate my dad," Cassie told the agent. "He stole from them!"

"We *will* catch them, Scott," Agent Woo said.

Agent Stoltz came downstairs. "Nothing up there," he said to his boss, and they left.

Scott loved his weekends with his daughter. Cassie was smart, funny, and warm. Cassie and her mom, Maggie, didn't live with Scott now. Maggie had a new husband. But they were all good friends.

"Tell me about Captain America again, Dad," Cassie said.

"Again? O.K. ... The Avengers had a big fight in Germany, and Captain America called me. I know that I'm not as good as him ..."

"Dad! *He* helps people. *You* help people!" Cassie shouted. "You're Ant-Man!"

"I *was* Ant-Man," Scott said. "Hank doesn't want me to be Ant-Man again."

"And what happened in Germany?" asked Cassie.

"I had a fight with Iron Man," Scott answered.

Cassie knew the story well. "And then, you didn't shrink," she laughed. "You were a *giant* Ant-Man! Everybody saw you on T.V.!"

"Yes," said Scott. "That was a mistake."

"The FBI saw your suit and knew ... Hank made that suit. Now, they want to arrest Hank?"

"That's it, Cassie," Scott said. "I feel really bad about that."

Then, Maggie arrived. It was the end of Cassie's weekend with her dad.

"Only three more days! Then, we can see you *outside* your house," Maggie said excitedly to Scott. She took Cassie home.

Three days? That's easy! Scott thought.

Scott made little birds out of paper, he played games, and he played music. He worked on plans for his new job with Luis at their tech company, X-Con. Luis was his friend in prison, and his best friend now.

When Scott fell asleep that evening, in his head he was in his Ant-Man suit again, in the Quantum Realm. But this time, he could see ... Janet van Dyne! Then, suddenly, he was in a strange house and a woman spoke through his mouth.

"I'm going to find you," the woman said.

He moved through the house to a bedroom. There was a child's closet in there, with horses on the door. A little girl was inside. She was about seven, younger than Cassie.

"There you are!" said the woman.

"You always find me, Mom," the girl laughed, and looked at Scott.

Mom? thought Scott. But then, he understood. In that house, in his head, he wasn't Scott. He was *Janet!*

Suddenly, he woke up. *Now, I'll* have *to speak to Hank*, he thought.

He couldn't wait three days. He found a phone in the back of his closet. He phoned Hank, but there was no answer.

"Hi, Hank," he said into the phone. "I know that you don't want to hear from me. But in my sleep, I saw some strange things. I think I saw your wife in the Quantum Realm. And then, it got stranger—then, I *was* your wife."

That sounds stupid, Scott thought. He broke the phone in two and threw it away.

Later, he sat down in front of the T.V. in his night clothes.

BZZZZ! There was a wasp in the room, and it flew around him. Then, it sat on his face. "*OW!*" he cried. Slowly, his eyes closed and he fell asleep.

When Scott woke up the next morning, he was in a car, in the same clothes. He looked at the driver. It was Hope! Hope van Dyne, Hank's daughter.

"Am I asleep?" he asked.

Hope didn't answer him. *She* had questions for *him*.

"Did you really see my mom down there?" she asked.

"I don't know," Scott said slowly. And then, "I can't be here! I'm under house arrest! I have to get home."

He tried the car door, but he couldn't open it.

"I shrank the car, Scott. The doors don't open when we're ant size."

"Take me home," Scott said unhappily. "When the FBI come to the house, I have to be there."

"They won't visit you," Hope said. "They think you're at home. One of Dad's giant ants is sitting at your breakfast table and wearing your tracker around one of its legs. It's being *you*. That means nine hours in bed, five hours each day in front of the T.V., and two hours in the bathroom."

"I am *never* in the bathroom for two hours," Scott said. "And how do you know about my day? Are you watching me?"

"Yes," Hope answered. "When something can hurt us, we watch it. You're dangerous, so we watch you."

She drove through a tunnel.

"I'm sorry about Germany," Scott said. "Cap called me. He really wanted my help."

"Cap?" Hope repeated.

"Captain America," said Scott. "His friends call him Cap. I'm sorry. I didn't think about you and Hank ..."

Hope laughed, but it wasn't a happy laugh. "You didn't think about a lot of things," she said.

"How is Hank?" Scott asked.

"Running from the FBI. We lost the house, we can't stay in one location. How do you *think* he is?"

"I'm sorry," Scott said again.

"Forget it," Hope said angrily. "I'm not interested. I'm only talking to you because you saw Mom."

They stopped outside an old office building. Nobody worked there. The windows were dirty, and there was no company name above the door.

WHOOSH! Hope made the car full size, and they got out. Inside, they went up two floors and came out into a very large laboratory.

"You'll be home before lunch."

"*WOW!*" said Scott. In the middle of the lab was a giant tunnel. There were giant ants, too—they worked busily all around the lab. At one end of the tunnel was a pod. And behind the pod was Hank Pym.

Hank closed his computer.

"Listen, Hank," Scott started to say. "I'm ..."

Hank stopped him. "I don't want to hear it," he said, and then he spoke to Hope. "Can we start?"

"Yes," Hope said, and she turned to Scott. "This is two years' work. When *you're* watching T.V., *we're* working! It's a tunnel to the Quantum Realm."

Scott looked at Hope with wide eyes.

"To my mom," she continued. "We don't think she's dead. We think she's down there. Now, we have to find her location. And we think *that* is inside your head. I'm going to take the pod down there, and bring her home."

"We powered up the tunnel last night for the first time," Hank said. "For a very short time, the doorway to the Quantum Realm opened. Then, the tunnel closed again."

"And ...?" Scott asked.

"And," Hope said, "five minutes later, *you* called. With your story about Mom."

"So you think …?"

"When the door opened, she spoke to us through you."

"That's crazy," said Scott.

"No," said Hank angrily. "It's *not* crazy. You stole an Ant-Man suit from me. You went to Germany with the Avengers and you didn't tell us. *That* was crazy. Who has my suit now?"

"Nobody has your suit, Hank," Scott said. "I threw it away."

"That was my life's work," Hank shouted. "You threw it away?"

"I'm sorry," Scott repeated. "And last night I didn't see Janet in the Quantum Realm. She was in a house with a little girl."

"What?" said Hope. "Who was the little girl? Was it Cassie?"

"No," Scott answered.

"*Where* was the little girl?" Hope asked quickly.

"She was in a closet," Scott said. "Janet found her there."

"Was the closet red?" asked Hope. "With horses on it?"

"Yes," Scott said slowly.

"That was me, when I was seven!" Hope said. She turned to Hank. "It's her!"

"I knew it!" Hank shouted.

"We have to get that part from Burch," Hope said quickly. "Let's go."

"*What* part?" Scott asked. "Who's Burch?"

"Sonny Burch sells us tech for the lab," Hope answered. "We have to get one more part from him. Then, our tunnel will stay open."

Hank took a box from his desk. Outside, Hope took a bag from their car and threw it to Scott.

"Here are your clothes," she said. "You can change on the way."

Hank had a small controller in his hand. *WHOOSH!* The car shrank to ant size, and Hank put it in the box. He took a small van out of the box

and put it on the road. *WHOOSH!* The van was now full size, and Hank opened the door.

Scott didn't want to get in. "Listen," he said. "Of course I want to help you—you know that. But I have to be home when the FBI come. I can't go to prison for twenty years."

"Scott, it'll be fine," said Hope. "We'll get the part and put it in the tunnel. Mom will tell you her location. You'll tell us. Then, you'll be home before lunch."

"O.K., fine," said Scott. "But can I wait in the lab?"

WHOOSH! Hank shrank the lab to the size of a sports bag. He put it in the van.

Somebody in a white suit watched them from across the street. Who—or what—was it? One minute you could see it. The next minute you couldn't. Was it a ghost?

Hope drove to the center of town and stopped near an expensive hotel. She left Scott and Hank in the van, and walked into the hotel restaurant.

"Ah, Susan!" a man called. He wore an expensive suit and sat at a table. His men stood behind him. The man's name was Sonny Burch, and he bought and sold technology parts. He didn't always *buy* them; his men often stole them for him. "But no, Susan's not your name. I have a good friend at the FBI. I pay him and he tells me things. I know now that you're Hope van Dyne. And you're working with Hank Pym, your father."

"Do you have the part, Sonny?" Hope asked coldly.

"I do," he said, but he didn't move.

This wasn't good. Hope put a small bag on the table and showed him

Hank shrank the lab to the size of a sports bag.

the money. Scott and Hank watched from the van. Hope sat down at the table and looked Sonny in the eye.

"What are you building with these parts?" Sonny asked the question, and then he answered it. "Quantum technology. And what's the next big thing? Where's the smart money going? Into quantum technology."

"So what do you want?" Hope asked.

"I have some buyers for your lab," Sonny said. "And they'll pay a lot of money."

"Thank you, Sonny," Hope said. "But we aren't interested. So I'll take the part ..."

Hope put her hand out for the part, but Sonny stopped her.

"My buyers won't take no for an answer," he said.

"O.K. I'll say goodbye," Hope said. She stood up and tried to take her bag of money. Again, Sonny stopped her.

"*You* can go," Sonny said. "Your money is staying here."

Hope walked away. Sonny stood up, and he and his men started to leave the restaurant.

CRASH! A table suddenly flew across the room and hit some of Sonny's men. *BZZZZ!* A small wasp flew around them. Suddenly, it was the same size as them. It was Hope—The Wasp. *THUMP!* She kicked the first man and jumped into the second man. *POW!* She hit the third man and flew into a fourth. Then, she shrank again and flew above their heads. *BANG! BANG!* The men shot at her with their guns, but she was too quick and too small.

Sonny gave the part and the money to one of his men. "Go!" he shouted, and the man ran through the restaurant kitchen. The Wasp was behind him. The fight continued, with kitchen knives, plates, and vegetables.

With her strong powers, The Wasp was too good for Sonny's men. She

took the part and the bag of money. She walked through the restaurant, and put Sonny's money on the table again.

"Thanks for the part," she said to Sonny. He was very angry—he couldn't speak.

She was at the door when she saw something in a white suit. It was there, and then it wasn't there. The Wasp stopped. *WHOOSH!* It was in her face. She tried to hit it, but now it was behind her.

"Dad," she said into her radio, "are you seeing this?"

"Hope, get out of there," Hank shouted in her ear.

ZAM! Suddenly, the ghost threw Hope onto a table. The part fell to the floor. Hope kicked a chair at the ghost.

Scott watched from the van. "I have to do something," he said, and opened the door.

"Wait!" cried Hank, and opened a box. Inside was an Ant-Man suit. "This is a new suit," he said. "It isn't ready, but it works ... most of the time. Take it."

In the hotel, The Wasp tried to take the part from the ghost. Suddenly, Ant-Man was there, and he kicked the ghost across the floor.

"You taught me that kick," Ant-Man said to The Wasp. "Remember? What happened to us?"

"This is not the time for a conversation, Scott," The Wasp said.

They looked for the ghost, but it wasn't there. And the part wasn't there.

"Dad?" The Wasp said.

"Nothing here," Hank said. But then, there was a strange noise in The Wasp's ear. *ZZZHHH!*

"*DAD!*" The Wasp shouted, and ran to the van. "Are you O.K.?"

"No!" Hank shouted. "That ghost—it took the lab!"

ZAM! Suddenly, the ghost threw Hope onto a table.

"You're with her?"

Hope drove fast.

"What *was* that?" she said to the others.

"I don't know," said Hank. "But we have to find the lab."

"Where's the lab's tracker?" asked Scott.

"Somebody turned it off," Hank told him.

"There's quantum energy in the lab, right?" Hope said. "Can we follow that quantum energy? Do we have the tech?"

"Yes, but ..."

"... it's in the lab," Scott said.

"I know! Let's ask Bill Foster. He'll have that tech."

"Great!" said Scott. And then, "Who's Bill Foster?"

"Dad worked with Bill at S.H.I.E.L.D. for years," Hope told him.

"Bill won't have the right tech," said Hank. "And he won't give it to *me* ..."

"Dad," Hope said. "We don't have any other ideas! We have to try ..."

The ghost in the white suit arrived at an old house in the woods. It carried Hank's lab and the part inside, into a large room full of machines.

The ghost took off its suit; inside was a young woman. She looked very sick. She opened the door to a glass box and almost fell onto a bed inside.

ZZZHHH! The lights came on in the box. Lines of yellow energy jumped over the girl. She closed her eyes and started to feel better.

Bill Foster taught quantum technology in San Francisco. Scott, Hope, and Hank wore dark glasses and hats, and walked carefully past the cameras.

"It's too open here," said Scott quietly.

"Nobody will see us," Hank answered.

They found Bill in his office and told him about their problem.

"I'm sorry," Bill said. "I don't have that old tech now."

"I knew it!" said Hank.

In the past, Hank and Bill worked in the same lab. Bill knew as much as Hank about quantum technology—but they were not friends.

"Hank is a very difficult man," Bill told Scott. "I couldn't work with him, so I left."

"You left!" Hank laughed. "I remember it differently!"

"Everything is about *him*!" Bill told Scott. "Only one person could work with him—and that was Janet. And what happened to *her*?"

Hank ran across the room. He wanted to hit Bill. Hope and Scott quickly jumped between them.

Suddenly, Scott saw something through the office window. "The FBI are here!" he shouted.

Agent Woo looked up at Bill's window. When he and his men started to move, Scott was half-way out of the door, with Hank and Hope behind him.

"Why don't you try one of the old Ant-Man suits?" Bill called after them. "Maybe it can find the lab for you."

"That's a good idea," Hope said. "Thank you, Bill." And she ran with the others.

Agent Woo and his men quickly arrived in Bill's office.

"Mr. Foster," Agent Woo said. "The cameras showed Hank Pym and Hope van Dyne in the square outside. Where are they?"

"I was around thirty years old when I saw Hank Pym for the last time," Bill said. "He never visits me."

"Why not?" Agent Woo asked.

"Because he hates me and I hate him," Bill told him.

Hank drove the van across the bridge into the city.

"Bill never had one good idea," he said.

"Maybe his idea about the old Ant-Man suit will work," said Hope.

"O.K., *one* good idea," Hank said. "But we don't *have* an old suit. Somebody in this van threw the last one away in Germany!" He looked angrily at Scott.

"You know, life's strange ..." Scott said.

"Oh!" said Hope excitedly. "*You have the suit!* You brought it home from Germany."

"What!" Hank shouted.

"It was your life's work, Hank!" Scott said. "I *had* to bring it back." Hope laughed. "Before I came home, I shrank the suit. I mailed it to Luis."

"You sent my suit through the mail?"

"It's fine," said Scott. "Let's go and get it. Now, it's ... er ... at the bottom of Cassie's school bag. She doesn't know it's there. Who's going to look for it there?"

Hank was very angry, but he drove to Cassie's school. Scott and Hope put their suits on and flew in. Hank was right—the new Ant-Man suit wasn't ready. First, Ant-Man shrank, and then he was a giant. One minute he was too small, the next minute he was too big.

"I can't control this thing," he told Hope.

But he found the old Ant-Man suit in Cassie's school bag. Then, in the back of the van, Hank tried the tracker technology from the old suit. It worked! It showed them the location of the lab.

They followed the tracker to an old house in the woods. It was dark, but there were lights in the house. Hank stayed in the van.

Scott loved working with Hope again. "It's like the old days!" he said.

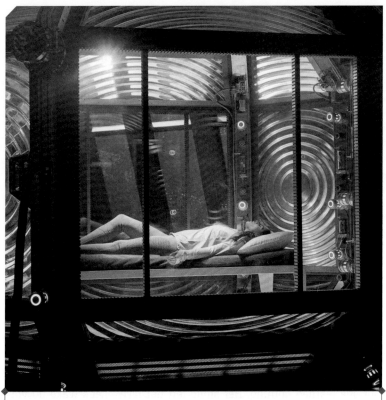

They saw the young woman on the bed in the glass box, asleep

"You're right," said Hope. "But ... Germany. Why didn't you invite me, too?"

"Did you *want* to come to Germany?"

"You'll never know. But I know one thing. You're under house arrest because you *didn't* ask me."

Ant-Man called a flying ant. They flew inside the house and into ... the ghost? But it was only the suit. There was nobody inside it. They saw the young woman on the bed in the glass box, asleep.

"Let's get out of here before she wakes up," The Wasp said. She and Ant-Man were now full size.

The lab and the part were on a table.

"Get the lab, Scott," said The Wasp. But when she looked again at the glass box, the girl wasn't there.

Oh, no! she thought. Too late. *POW!* Ghost hit her on the back of her head.

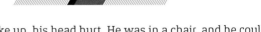

When Scott woke up, his head hurt. He was in a chair, and he couldn't move his hands. Hope and Hank were next to him, but their eyes were closed.

WHOOSH! The young woman suddenly stood in front of him.

"Hi. I'm Ava," she said. She smiled at him.

"Oh! I'm Scott," he answered. "You're not wearing your suit. You can go through things ... without the suit?"

"Yes," she said. "But it hurts more when I don't wear the suit. The suit helps to control my powers."

She smiled again and came nearer.

"Are you going to kill me?" he asked.

"No, Scott," she said. "I'm not going to kill you. I know that you know Janet's location." She wanted to put her hands on his head, but her hands went through him. She wanted to find Janet's location, inside his head, but she learned nothing. Her smile left her face. "Let's wake up your friends," she said angrily.

First, she kicked the back of Hope's chair hard, and then Hank's chair.

"Dad, are you O.K.?" Hope asked. Then, she spoke to Ava. "Do *not* do that again."

"I think, Hope, I'm being very kind to Dr. Pym."

"What are you talking about?" Hank asked.

But Ava didn't answer. A man came into the light. "Hank hurt many people when he was at S.H.I.E.L.D.," the man said. "Ava is one of them." It was Bill Foster.

"You're with *her?*" Scott asked. "Aren't you with *us?*"

"What does Bill mean?" Hope asked her father.

Ava answered. "My father was Elihas Starr, a scientist. He worked with Dr. Pym at S.H.I.E.L.D.—on quantum science. But then, my father made a big mistake. He wanted to do things differently from the great Hank Pym." She turned to Hank. "But you didn't like that. So my father had to leave. He went to South America and started a new lab there. Then, something went wrong, and there was an accident. I was a child, and my mom and I were in the lab at the time. My mom and dad died in the accident. And me ... Every little part of me broke into atoms. Those atoms never stop moving inside me. And it hurts—it *really* hurts—all the time."

"I was at S.H.I.E.L.D. when I got the call from Argentina," Bill said. "I brought Ava home."

"Bill was kind," Ava said. "But other S.H.I.E.L.D. agents wanted to use me and my strange powers. I had to work for them. I stole for them, and I killed for them. But *they* didn't help *me*."

"When S.H.I.E.L.D. closed, Ava stayed with me," Bill told them. "I built the glass box for her. It gives her quantum energy, and that helps, but not

"When S.H.I.E.L.D. closed, Ava stayed with me," Bill told them. "I built the glass box for her."

much. She wanted to kill you, Hank. But I told her no. So she watched you, and she learned about the tunnel."

"Ava," Hank said kindly, "I want to help you."

"No, Hank," Bill said. "*I'm* going to help her."

"Oh, really?" Hank laughed. "How?"

"Janet," Ava said.

"Down there in the Quantum Realm," Bill said, "Janet is full of quantum energy. We can use some of her power for Ava and make Ava better."

"What!" Hank cried. "Are you crazy? That will break Janet in two! You'll kill her."

"You don't know that," said Bill. "We're going to power up your tunnel. Scott's going to tell us Janet's location. Or I'm going to call the FBI."

"You'll kill Janet!" Hank shouted. He wanted to move his arms, but he couldn't. "*AGH!*" Suddenly, he fell onto Hope and his eyes closed.

"Help! Bill!" Hope said. "Dad isn't well. Give me that box. Now!"

"Which box?" Bill asked.

"The red box ... on the table," Hope shouted.

"Wait!" Ava shouted, suddenly. "Don't open it!"

But she was too late.

"Where is Scott Lang?"

Ten giant ants jumped out of Hank's red box. They ran at Ava and Bill, and cut Scott free from his chair. He helped Hope and Hank. They took the lab and the machine part, and ran out to the van.

There wasn't much time now. They drove a short way, and made the lab full size there in the woods. Hank and the ants—his helpers—moved around the machines and worked quickly.

"Ava is wrong," Hank said. "Elihas Starr stole my plans."

Hope put the new part in, and powered up the tunnel.

"Are you excited?" Scott asked her.

"Yes," said Hope. "I'm going to see my mom again. It's wonderful. But I'm a little afraid, too. Maybe she'll be a different person. Maybe she won't remember me!"

"When I was in prison," Scott said warmly, "I wanted only one thing. I wanted to see Cassie again. Your mom will be the same."

"Thank you, Scott," she said, and looked into his eyes. "I feel better now."

His phone started to play a happy song, and Hope laughed. It was Luis. He was at the office of their tech company, X-Con. Two men, Kurt and Dave, worked for them, and they were in the office with him. Luis had a problem with some work for an important customer.

"I have to see you … now!" he said to Scott on the phone. "We're meeting people from Karapetyan in the morning, and we aren't ready."

"It's difficult," Scott said. "I'm not at home."

"Where are you?" asked Luis. "I'll bring the work to you."

Luis turned off his phone, and put his papers in a bag.

"I'm taking these plans to Scott," he told Kurt and Dave. "I'll see you in the morning when we meet Karapetyan."

But before Luis could leave, Sonny Burch walked in with three of his men.

"Luis!" said Sonny. "I heard something interesting about you from somebody at the FBI. You're friends with Scott Lang and Hank Pym. I know that Hank Pym has a wonderful lab. I want that lab. Where is it?"

"I don't know anything about a lab," Luis said.

"Sit down, Luis," Sonny told him. "I have some dangerous friends, and they want that lab. We don't have all day. Uzman, my man here, has some truth serum in this box. He's going to give you some. It won't hurt. But you *will* remember and you *will* talk."

When the giant ants left Bill's house in the woods, Bill turned to Ava.

"We have to get that lab," he said. "Your glass box—and the suit—they aren't working very well."

"How long do I have?" asked Ava.

"Maybe two weeks," Bill told her sadly.

Ava put on her suit. "I'll find the lab," Ghost said.

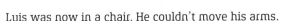

Luis was now in a chair. He couldn't move his arms.

"O.K., Luis. Where is Scott Lang?" Sonny asked.

It was an easy question. Luis started his answer at the beginning.

"When I first met Scott," he said, "he was not a happy man." He told Sonny about prison, about Maggie and Cassie ...

"Stop!" said Sonny. "I love a good story. But this is not the time."

"He loves to talk," said Dave.

"Right," said Luis. "So Scott came out of prison, and then he met Hope. She liked him. He liked her. You know the story. But then Captain America called Scott. He went to Germany. He didn't tell Hope. She was angry. She didn't want to see him again ..."

Luis talked for five more minutes about Hope, Germany, and their company's problems.

"What problems?" asked Kurt. He knew nothing about them. "Does X-Con have money problems?"

"Yes, it does," Luis said. The truth serum was very good. "I'm sorry. We *have to* get this Karapetyan job."

"*HEY!*" Sonny shouted at Kurt. "*I'm* asking the questions. Now, one more time. *WHERE IS SCOTT LANG?*"

"You mean, now?" Luis said. "In the woods."

"The woods?" said ... Ghost. Suddenly, she was in the room, too.

"*AGH!*" Everybody jumped back.

Ghost put her face close to Luis. "*Which* woods?"

Ghost put her face close to Luis.

"The Muir Woods," Luis said quickly. "Off the Panoramic Highway." Ghost ran through the wall of the office.

"No!" said Sonny. "She'll get there before us." Then, he had an idea. He took out his phone and called Agent Stoltz at the FBI. For money, Stoltz always told him everything. Sonny gave Stoltz a location for Scott, Hank, and Hope. "But listen," he said. "I want that lab. You get that for me."

"I understand, Mr. Burch," Stoltz said.

In the lab, the tunnel was ready. Hank started to power it up.

"When the tunnel's open, Scott," Hope said, "give us Janet's location."

Parts of the machine started to turn. The tunnel worked.

"Can you hear Janet in your head?" Hank asked Scott.

"No, nothing," Scott said.

"Let's wait a minute," Hank said. But then the parts started to move more slowly.

"No!" Hope shouted. "Why is this happening?"

"I don't know," Hank answered.

The machine stopped. Scott started to feel strange. He ran to the controls, and put in some new numbers.

"Get away from that, Scott!" Hank shouted.

"I'm sorry," Scott said. "I don't have much time. This isn't right."

Hope looked at her father. And then, Scott spoke again.

"After thirty years down here," Scott said—but he sounded like Janet—"I know I can do this."

Hank looked at Scott. "Janet?" he asked.

Scott turned and looked at Hank. He put his hand on Hank's face. "Hello, my love," he said, but now he *was* Janet. Then, he turned to Hope. "My little girl," he said lovingly.

"Mom?" Hope said.

"We have to be quick," Scott said. "Your work on this tunnel is great! There's only a very small mistake. There!" The tunnel started to work again!

"Janet," Hank said, "tell us your location. How do we find you?"

"I will be with you all the way. Listen to me, and follow me, O.K.? It's very dangerous, so be very careful. Time works differently in the Quantum Realm. You only have two hours. After that, it will be too late."

"We won't lose you, Mom," Hope said. "Not this time."

And then Scott was Scott again. He looked at Hank and Hope. He couldn't remember the last five minutes.

"No," he said. "I can't tell you anything. Janet isn't talking to me. Sorry!"

Hank smiled at Hope, and they ran to the pod. They got it ready quickly and told Scott about Janet inside his head.

Scott's phone played the happy song again. "It's Luis," he told Hope, and answered it.

"Are you coming?" Scott asked.

"Yes," said Luis. "But not only me. Also Ghost, the FBI, and Sonny Burch. They gave me some truth serum. After that, I couldn't stop talking. I'm sorry, Scott."

Oh, no, Scott thought. *Hope will be really angry with me this time.*

"We have to leave here," he told Hope.

"What?" Hope said. "We can't go. We have to find my mom."

"The FBI—they know that you're here. They're on their way."

"How do they know?" asked Hank.

"I told Luis our location," said Scott. "He and I have to work on the Karapetyan job."

"You *told* him? Are you *crazy*?" Hope cried.

"Scott!" Hank shouted.

They ran to the controls and turned off the tunnel.

"And there's one more thing," Scott said. "The FBI is coming to my house, so I have to go. Or it's twenty years in prison for me. Can I take the suit?"

Hank didn't answer him. He was too angry.

"Scott!" shouted Hope. "Go!"

"Follow the ants!"

Scott shrank down to ant size, and called one of Hank's ants. He jumped on its back, and they flew up into the sky.

At the same time, Cassie arrived at Scott's house with her mom. They wanted to get Cassie's sports shoes for school.

"Run upstairs and find your dad, Cassie," Maggie said.

"Dad?" Cassie called.

She heard the sound of bath water and called through the bathroom door. But when she opened the door, she saw a giant ant with a shower hat on its head. Cassie laughed.

Downstairs, the front door flew open, and Agent Woo came in with his agents.

"Where is he?" Agent Woo shouted.

"He's upstairs, in the bathroom," an agent told him. "I'm following his tracker."

Cassie stood on the stairs, in Agent Woo's way.

"Dad's sick," she told him.

"Is he *really?*" Agent Woo asked. "Move away, Cassie."

The FBI man pushed past Cassie. Suddenly, the bathroom door opened, and Scott came out. He was in his night clothes.

"Agent Woo?" he asked. "What are *you* doing here?"

Cassie smiled behind Agent Woo's back.

"Scott?" Agent Woo said.

"Sorry," Scott said, on his way into the bathroom again. "I have to go. I'm really sick."

"I told you," Cassie said to Agent Woo.

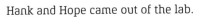

Hank and Hope came out of the lab.

"Let's get in the van," Hank said.

WHOOSH! He shrank the lab down. Behind the lab, there were 100 men with guns.

"Hands up!" they shouted.

Some FBI cars arrived, and Agent Stoltz jumped out of one.

WHOOSH! He shrank the lab down. Behind the lab, there were 100 men with guns.

"Hank Pym. Hope van Dyne. You are under arrest," said Stoltz.

His agents took them away.

Agent Stoltz took the lab, and quietly moved away from the other FBI agents. He put it in the back of his car, ready for Sonny Burch. *POW!* Something hit Stoltz hard in the stomach, and he fell to the ground. It was Ghost. She took the lab and ran into the woods.

Scott and Cassie sat on the floor in Scott's living room.

"You really helped me with Agent Woo," Scott told his daughter. "Thanks."

"That's O.K.," Cassie said. "You're Ant-Man again. You didn't tell me."

"I know. I'm sorry," Scott said. "I'm always doing stupid things. And who gets hurt? You, Cassie."

"But you're *helping* people," she said. "*That's* not stupid."

"I make mistakes every time," he said.

"Hope's smart. Why don't you work with her?"

"She's angry with me," Scott told her.

"And are you going to go and help her?" Cassie asked.

"I can't help her," Scott said, "because I don't want to hurt *you*."

"You can do it," said Cassie. "I know you can."

Scott put his arms around his daughter.

"You can do it," said Cassie. "I know you can."

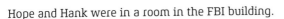

Hope and Hank were in a room in the FBI building.

"Agent Woo will see you in an hour," an agent said.

"An hour?" Hank shouted. "We don't *have* an hour."

The agent closed the door. There were cameras in the room.

"What now?" Hank asked. "There are 100 or more agents in the building ..."

"... all with guns," Hope said. "But we have to do *something*."

Suddenly, there were ants everywhere. They walked over the cameras, so the agents outside could see nothing. Then, suddenly, on the table were Hope's Wasp suit, and for Hank, dark glasses, an FBI jacket, and a hat.

Hope looked up. "Scott?" she said. "Where are you?"

"Outside, in the van. What are you two waiting for?" Ant-Man said. They could hear him through The Wasp suit.

Hank put on the FBI clothes, and walked quickly out of the building. The Wasp flew next to his ear. They climbed into the van.

The Wasp smiled at Ant-Man, and he smiled back.

"Hi," he said.

"Excuse me!" called Hank from the back of the van. "There'll be 100 FBI agents with guns on the street in about one minute. Don't smile at my daughter—drive!"

A little way down the street, Burch's men watched. Uzman called Burch. "They're out," he said.

"I'm on my way," Burch answered.

Inside the building, Agent Woo was very angry. "How could this happen?" he shouted.

"How do we find the lab?" Scott asked.

"After we lost it the first time," Hank said, "I put a new tracker into it. Look up at the sky and follow the ants!"

In the sky above them, flying ants showed them the way. Scott drove fast through the city. They turned into a small road and went under a bridge. There was the lab.

Inside the lab, Bill and Ava worked quickly.

"Listen, Ava," Bill said. "Maybe this is too dangerous. Let's wait."

"Wait?" Ava cried. "I have days before I die. And you want me to wait! We're doing this, Bill. Now! Power up the tunnel."

Outside the lab, Scott, Hope, and Hank made a plan.

"One, we have to get into that lab," Scott said. "Two, we have to kick out Foster and Ghost. Three, we'll have to *fight* Ghost."

"You two can fight Ghost and watch the tunnel," Hank said. "*I'm* going down in the pod, to the Quantum Realm. I have to go quickly, before Janet changes her location! And then, the lab has to be full size, or we can't leave the Realm."

"Wait?" Ava cried. "I have days before I die."

"You cannot leave here."

Suddenly, a second van stopped next to them. The driver was Luis. Hope looked at Scott.

"He's going to help us," Scott said. "I asked him."

They got ready. Scott went up to the third floor of an old office building next to the lab. He watched from a window. Hope and Luis waited in the van. Hank called his friends, the ants.

Inside the lab, the tunnel stopped. Something was wrong.

"What's happening?" Ava asked.

"I don't know," Bill said. And then, they saw them. Giant ants were everywhere.

Ava went outside in her Ghost suit. She saw a long line of ants, and she followed them to the old office building.

In the lab, the giant ants were all around Bill. He couldn't move. Hank followed them inside.

"Hank, I wanted to help Ava. She's going to die and she's afraid," Bill said.

"After I get Janet, I'll help Ava," Hank said. He put on a suit for his trip to the Quantum Realm. "We'll think of something."

"I hope you find Janet," Bill said. "I hope you bring her back."

"Thank you, Bill," Hank said, and smiled. "Now, please go outside. The ants will show you the way."

The ants pushed Bill through the doors. Hank climbed into the pod and turned everything on.

"You have fifteen minutes," the pod said. "Repeat. You have fifteen minutes."

The Wasp spoke loudly to Ant-Man through his suit.

"Can you see her?" she asked.

"No, nothing," Ant-Man answered. And then, Ghost was behind him. *BANG!* She pushed his head into the window. *ZAM!* She kicked him in the stomach. *CRASH!* He flew across the room into a wall.

Ant-Man pushed the controls on his suit. He wanted to shrink. But they didn't work ... again.

"Call the ants away from the lab, Scott," Ghost said.

He turned and ran through the dark offices. He jumped on desks and kicked over chairs. Ghost stayed close behind him.

"What's happening, Hope?" Ant-Man called. "I have some bad ghost problems here."

The pod moved into the tunnel.

"I'm ready to go down," Hank told his daughter from inside the pod. "I love you, Hope."

"You'll come back, Dad," she said. "I can't lose you, too."

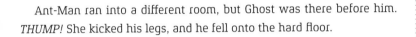

Ant-Man ran into a different room, but Ghost was there before him. *THUMP!* She kicked his legs, and he fell onto the hard floor.

The tunnel opened. The pod moved fast, with Hank inside. *WHOOSH!* It shrank down to subatomic size. It went through smaller and smaller worlds. Then, it arrived in the Quantum Realm.

"I'm coming, Janet," Hank told his wife.

"Now!" The Wasp shouted. *WHOOSH!* She shrank the lab. Ghost stopped fighting Ant-Man, and they watched from the office window. Luis jumped out of the van and took the lab.

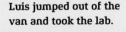

Luis jumped out of the van and took the lab.

Ghost looked at Ant-Man. "Sorry, Ghost," he said. "You had to be out of the way."

The Wasp drove away, fast.

"No!" Ghost shouted.

Then, Ant-Man shrank to ant size, and followed the van on a flying ant.

But suddenly, The Wasp had to stop. A line of cars was in front of her, across the road.

"Really?" she said angrily. "This man again!"

It was Sonny Burch, with his men.

"We have a change of plan," The Wasp called to Ant-Man. *SCREECH!* She turned the van around very quickly.

"*WHOAH!*" cried Luis.

Sonny and his men drove after them.

"I want that lab, boys," he said on his radio.

One of Sonny's cars tried to push The Wasp's van off the road. But she suddenly went faster, and the car hit a wall. *CRASH!*

Another of Sonny's cars was behind her.

"It's going to hit us," Luis shouted. "We're going to die."

WHOOSH! The Wasp quickly shrank the van down to ant size, and drove it under the car. Then, she pushed a control, and it was full size again. It threw the car high into the sky. *BANG!* The car came down again and hit the road.

But Sonny had more men and more cars ...

In the Quantum Realm, the pod lost power. Hank tried the radio, but there was no answer. He couldn't talk to the lab because it wasn't full size. It was in Hope's van.

"What are they doing up there?" asked Hank angrily. He tried all the controls.

"Please wait," the pod said to him.

Hank looked at the subatomic world around him. Everything was very beautiful, and the colors were wonderful. Small things looked like giant

Small things looked like giant animals here.

animals here. He could hear ghostly sounds and calls.

"Please wait," the pod said again.

But then, one of the strange animals came and opened its mouth wide. It wanted to eat the pod.

Suddenly, Hank had full power. "We are ready," said the pod. He drove away fast from the animal's open mouth.

Ant-Man flew down into Hope's van. He was full size now.

"You drive," The Wasp said, and they changed places. There was a box of candy on the floor of the van. The Wasp opened the back door and threw it out. She pushed a control on her suit. *WHAM!* Suddenly, the box was giant size. It hit one of Sonny's men and threw him on the road.

But then, somebody was on top of the van—it was Ghost! She pulled open the van door and jumped in. *THUMP!* First, she kicked The Wasp out of the van. Then, she took the lab and jumped onto another van. She pushed the driver out of the door and sat in his place.

Quickly, Ant-Man had to drive around the man on the road. *CRASH!* He hit a car.

Sonny was in a car behind. "Get the lab!" he shouted to his men.

The Wasp watched from above, and followed Ghost. Then, she flew down to the van and jumped in next to Ghost. They started to fight.

Ant-Man called an ant. He wanted to help The Wasp. The ant put Scott down on the front window of Ghost's van. Quickly, Ant-Man pushed the control on his suit. Now he wasn't ant size. He was a giant! Ghost looked at him. *POW!* He hit her through the glass. The Wasp took the lab, but not for long. *CRASH!* Sonny's car drove into the back of Ghost's van. *WHEEE!* The lab flew out and Sonny caught it. *VROOM!* He and his men drove away fast.

The Wasp and Ghost fell on the ground. They got up and followed Sonny.

Ant-Man was on the moving van, but there was no driver now. "Where are you?" The Wasp said in his ear. "We don't have much time!"

"I'm on my way," he shouted.

In the Quantum Realm, Hank went down and down. First, it was very dark, and there was no sound. Then, the pod went faster and faster, before it stopped on an ocean of strange colors. Hank looked at the clock. He only had four minutes.

Sonny was on the phone again. "We don't have the controller for the lab," he shouted to his men. "We can't make it full size without the controller. It's in Hope's van!"

Luis was in Hope's van.

"Hope," he called on the radio. "Don't you want the controller for the lab? I have it here."

"Bring it to us, fast," The Wasp answered.

"But I can't drive the van. I can't start it," said Luis.

"There's a box of cars," Ant-Man shouted, "in the van. Use one of those. The controller will make it big."

Luis was very happy when he looked in the box of cars. He took out a purple sports car.

When Sonny's men arrived, Luis was in the sports car. *VROOM!* He drove quickly away.

Everybody was on their way through the city to the ocean. The Wasp was wasp size and flew. Ant-Man was giant size and ran. Ghost went through houses and offices. Luis was in the fast car, and Sonny and his men were behind him.

Ant-Man caught Sonny's car, and kicked it hard. *CRASH!* It hit a wall. Sonny jumped out with the lab and ran. Scott couldn't follow him because he was too big. His suit control didn't work—again!

There were a lot of people by the water. Some were very afraid when they saw Ant-Man. Some took photos. Most of them ran away. And then, Ant-Man saw Sonny.

Sonny was on a boat. A lot of other people were on it, too. The boat was out on the water, on a trip around the city. Ant-Man had to follow. *SPLASH!* He jumped in and swam after the boat.

"*AGH!*" cried the people on the boat when Ant-Man stood up next to it. "Help!"

Ant-Man took the lab from Sonny with his giant hand.

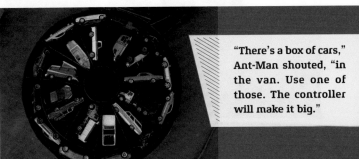

"There's a box of cars," Ant-Man shouted, "in the van. Use one of those. The controller will make it big."

Hank got out of the pod carefully. He could walk on the ocean of strange colors. This was Janet's location, but he couldn't see her. He felt very strange.

And then, there was somebody in the dark. He couldn't see the person's face. Suddenly, he felt hands on his head, and power from those hands ran into him. He closed his eyes and was very afraid.

He opened his eyes slowly. He really was in the Quantum Realm! The person in front of him really was Janet!

"It's me," she said. "I'm thirty years older, but it's me!"

They smiled and cried. She put her arms around him.

"I'm sorry," he said to his wife.

"You're here now," she said. "Let's go home."

They climbed into the pod.

"That power from your hands ..." he asked. "How did you do that?"

"This place changes you," she told him.

And then, the pod spoke to them. "We cannot find the location of the lab," it said. "You cannot leave here. Repeat. You cannot leave here."

Janet looked at Hank.

"They're having problems up there," he said.

The person in front of him really was Janet!

"Janet will die!"

Ant-Man walked slowly to dry ground, and carefully put the lab down. Luis arrived in the sports car, with The Wasp next to him.

"Oh, no!" said The Wasp when she saw the giant Ant-Man. "He's too big. He'll get tired." Ant-Man could only stay giant size for a short time before he fell asleep. His eyes started to close, and—*SPLASH!*—he fell back into the water.

"No!" The Wasp cried. "Take the lab," she said to Luis. "I have to help Scott." She flew to the water and swam down to Ant-Man.

Luis got out of the car, but Ghost was too quick for him. She took the lab and the controller.

WHOOSH! She made the lab full size. It pushed everything out of its way, and people ran for their lives.

In the Quantum Realm, the pod spoke: "The lab is full size," it said. "You can now leave. Repeat. You can now leave."

Hank smiled at Janet. "They did it," he said.

"Let's go and see our daughter," Janet said.

Ant-Man was asleep on the ocean floor. The Wasp pushed the size control on his suit. It didn't work. She opened it and made some changes. Then, it worked. Ant-Man shrank from giant to ant size.

Now, The Wasp couldn't see him in the dirty water. "Where are you, Scott?" she shouted. And then, she found him. "I have you!" Happily, she caught him in her hand and swam up again.

When they were on dry ground, she made him Scott size.

"Scott, wake up!" she shouted. He opened his eyes. "Oh!" she said. "You're not dead!" She threw her arms around him.

Outside the lab, Sonny and his men wanted to kill Luis.

"Don't shoot!" he said.

The men smiled ... and then—*ZAP!*—they fell to the ground. Behind them were Kurt and Dave. Luis hit Sonny, and then called the police.

"Now, where's that truth serum?" asked Luis.

Ghost powered up her glass box inside the lab. Bill came in.

"Ava!" he called. "I think Hank's right. Take quantum energy from Janet, and she'll die!"

"Oh, that's right," Ghost shouted back. "Think about *Janet*, not *me!*"

"She's a very smart scientist," Bill said. "Maybe she can help you."

"I don't have time for this," Ghost said. "Maybe Janet *will* die. I'm sorry

but I really hurt."

"No, I'm sorry, Ava," Bill said. "We have to find another way."

CRASH! Ghost threw Bill across the floor.

"*This* is the way," she said.

She pushed the controls on Hank's machines, and went into her glass box. "Give me your power, Janet," she said.

Down in the pod, Janet suddenly closed her eyes.

"Janet?" called Hank.

Quantum energy ran into Ghost's arms and legs, and made her stronger. At the same time, the energy left Janet, and made her weaker.

Ant-Man and The Wasp ran into the lab and turned off the machines.

"No!" shouted Ghost. *POW!* She came out of the glass box and fought The Wasp at the door to the quantum tunnel. *THUMP!* The pod started to arrive, and Ant-Man pushed The Wasp out of its way. Then, the door to the pod opened. Janet and Hank climbed out.

"Mom?" said Hope. She and her mother started to cry. "Life without you was ... very sad," Hope told her.

"I'm here now," Janet said. "We have time."

"Ms. Van Dyne," said Scott, "how do you do? I know that we met ... in my head!"

They laughed.

But then, everybody turned around because Ghost stood up. She wanted to fight again.

"Wait!" Janet said. She went to Ava. "You're hurting. I can feel it."

"I always hurt," said Ava, and she started to cry.

"I can help you," Janet told her.

She came out of the glass box and fought The Wasp at the door to the quantum tunnel.

Mom?" said Hope She and her mother started to cry.

She put her hands on Ava's head and closed her eyes. Energy from Janet ran into Ava. Bill watched.

Janet smiled. Ava opened and closed her hand. She could feel it! She put her hands on Janet, and she could feel *her*. Her hands didn't go through her.

BANG! The door to the lab opened suddenly, and Luis ran in.

"The FBI are coming!" he said.

"I have to go," Scott said.

"*We* have to go," said Hank.

Outside, Sonny Burch and his men sat on the ground, and Kurt and Dave watched them. Uzman's box was open next to them. There was no more truth serum in the bottle. Then, the police arrived.

"Put your hands up!" they shouted.

"You don't want *us*," said Kurt. "You want these men. They want to shoot people. We stopped them. They'll tell you everything!"

"We steal technology and sell it," said Uzman.

"We kill people every day," said another man.

"Mr. Burch—he's the boss," said Uzman.

"That's right, I am," said Sonny. "You have to send me to prison."

"My truth serum really works!" Uzman said.

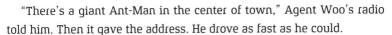

"There's a giant Ant-Man in the center of town," Agent Woo's radio told him. Then it gave the address. He drove as fast as he could.

SCREECH! He arrived and jumped out.

"I'm sorry, Scott, but we have you," he shouted up at the giant Ant-Man. "And on your last day of house arrest!"

The giant Ant-Man didn't move.

Down the street a little way, Scott—in his T-shirt—ran away quickly. Agent Woo didn't see him.

"Scott!" Agent Woo shouted to the Ant-Man suit. "Shrink!"

The suit shrank down to ant size—but Scott wasn't inside it.

"No!" Agent Woo shouted. He turned to his men. "We're going to Lang's house! Now!"

After they left, Hope flew down and took Scott's suit. She flew to her parents. They had the lab. Luis arrived in his van, and everybody jumped inside.

Ava and Bill were on a small street. They didn't want the police to see them.

"Leave me here," Ava told Bill.

"We'll be fine," Bill said.

"People are dead because of me," she said to Bill. "But you're a good man. Now, go!"

"I'm not leaving you," Bill told her.

Ava threw her arms around him.

SCREECH! Four FBI cars arrived at Scott's house at the same time. Agent Woo ran through the door, and his men followed.

They found Scott in the kitchen with a cup of coffee.

"Hi," he said. "Is this the end of my house arrest?"

Agent Woo looked at his men. They looked at him.

CLUNK! An agent took the tracker off Scott's leg.

"O.K., Scott," Agent Woo said. "You win this time."

The next day, Scott and Hope took Cassie to a drive-in movie theater. They watched the movie from the car and ate candy.

"Cassie," Hope said. "What do you want to be when you're older?"

"Dad helps people," Cassie answered. "I want to do that, too."

"Really?" Hope said, and she smiled at Scott.

"I wanted to work *with* him," Cassie said. "But he says that he wants *you.*"

"Is that right?" Hope said.

Weeks later, Ant-Man was on top of a building. Hope, Janet, and Hank were there, too.

"I was a top scientist," Hank said to his wife. "I had my name on buildings. Now, I have this."

There was a van and some computers. Inside the van was a tunnel—a *small* tunnel to the Quantum Realm.

Hope gave Ant-Man a bottle, and he went into the tunnel.

"O.K.," she said. "We're ready. We're going subatomic in five, four, three, two, one ..."

WHOOSH! Quantum energy pulled Ant-Man through the tunnel to the Quantum Realm. When he arrived, he opened the bottle. When it was full of quantum energy, he closed it again. It was for Ava.

"I have it," Ant-Man said into his radio.

"Great!" Hope answered. "We're bringing you home in five, four, three—"

Then, there was nothing.

"Haha. Very funny," Ant-Man said from the Quantum Realm. "Hello? Is anybody there?"

Activities

Chapter 1

Before you read

1 What do you know about ants? One of these sentences is wrong. Which one?

 a Ants are one of the strongest animals in the world, for their size.
 b Some of them can fly.
 c They have eight legs.
 d Ants don't have ears. They listen with their feet.

2 Talk to a friend. Do you know the story of *Ant-Man and The Wasp*? What does the picture on the front of this book tell you about them?

3 Look at the Word List at the back of the book. Then <u>underline</u> the best words in *italics* below.

 a My uncle is very tall. Next to me, he is a *ghost / giant*.
 b When something shrinks, it gets *bigger / smaller*.
 c My mom usually wears a *suit / tracker* to work.
 d The train traveled *under / through* the tunnel.
 e The police *stole / arrested* the two men when they came out of the bank.
 f An *ant / atom* is smaller than an *ant / atom*.

4 Read Who's Who? and the Introduction, and answer these questions.

 a Why can't Scott leave home when he wants?
 b What did Hope teach Scott?
 c Where is Hope's mother?
 d What happened to Ava's parents?
 e Where did Scott meet Luis for the first time?
 f Who knows the location of Janet in the Quantum Realm?
 g What did Scott's wife do when he went to prison?
 h Why did Scott go to Germany?
 i How did Hope and Hank know that Scott was in Germany?

While you read

5 Are these sentences right (✔) or wrong (✗)?

a In 1987, Hank wanted to go inside the missile, but he couldn't. ◯
b The missile hit San Francisco. ◯
c Hope and Hank are going to build a tunnel to the Quantum Realm. ◯
d Cassie lives with her father. ◯
e Scott has two more years of house arrest. ◯
f Scott is under house arrest because he fought with some of the Avengers in Germany. ◯
g Scott sees Janet when he is asleep. ◯
h Hope comes to Scott's house because she is in love with him. ◯

After you read

6 What do you learn about Scott Lang in this chapter? Write three sentences about him. What do you learn about his life under house arrest? Write three sentences about it.

Chapters 2–3

Before you read

7 Discuss these questions. What do you think?

a Will Agent Woo find the giant ant in Scott's house?
b Will Hope and Hank learn Janet's location from Scott?

While you read

8 Put each name in one of the sentences below.

Susan   Hope   The Wasp   Hank
Ant-Man   Janet   Ghost   Sonny

a Hope and Hank don't think that .... is dead.
b Scott stole an Ant-Man suit from .... and took it to Germany.
c Inside Scott's head, Janet was with seven-year-old ....

d Hope and Hank buy parts for their quantum tunnel from
....

e .... is watching when Hank shrinks the lab.

f Sonny knows that Hope's name is not really ....

g .... gets the part for the lab from Sonny's men.

h .... helps The Wasp in the fight with Ghost.

9 <u>Underline</u> the right words in *italics*.

a The lab's tracker is *on / off*.

b Hank *thinks / doesn't think* that Bill Foster will help him.

c Bill *tells / doesn't tell* Agent Woo that Hank and Hope were in his office.

d Hank's Ant-Man suit is in *Cassie's school bag / Germany*.

e Scott *can / can't* control Hank's new suit.

f Ava *learns / doesn't learn* Janet's location from inside Scott's head.

g Ava's father died in an accident in *his lab / Hank Pym's lab* in Argentina.

h Ava wants to *go to the Quantum Realm / get quantum energy from Janet*.

After you read

10 Work with another student. Discuss these questions.

a Do you think Dr. Pym is a kind man? Why (not)?

b Was S.H.I.E.L.D. kind to Ava after her parents died?

Chapters 4–5

Before you read

11 What do you think will happen when Bill opens the red box?

While you read

12 Who is speaking? Who are they talking to?

a "I'm going to see my mom again."

.... to ....

b "I'll bring the work to you."

.... to ....

c "How long do I have?"

.... to ....

d "Where is Scott Lang?"

.... to ....

e "Your work on this tunnel is great!"

.... to ....

f "Janet isn't talking to me."

.... to ....

g "They gave me some truth serum."

.... to ....

13 **Are these sentences right (✔) or wrong (✘)?**

   a Cassie sees a giant ant in a shower hat and laughs. ◯
   b Agent Woo sees a giant ant in a shower hat and is angry. ◯
   c Men with guns are waiting for Hank and Hope outside the lab. ◯
   d Ghost kicks Sonny Burch in the stomach and takes the lab. ◯
   e Scott sends ants into the FBI building. ◯
   f Hank dresses as an FBI agent, and Agent Woo arrests him. ◯
   g Scott, Hope, and Hank follow the ants to the lab. ◯

After you read

14 **Work with another student. Answer these questions.**

   a How does Scott get to his house before Agent Woo opens the bathroom door?
   b How do Hope and Hank get out of the FBI building?
   c Why doesn't Ava want to wait before they power up the tunnel?
   d Who is going to the Quantum Realm to get Janet?

Chapters 6–7

Before you read

15 **Will Hank get to the Quantum Realm? What do you think will happen there?**

While you read

16 What happens first? Number these sentences, 1–6.

    a Ant-Man takes the lab from Sonny.   ....

    b Hank starts to move through the tunnel to the
    Quantum Realm.   ....

    c The Wasp shrinks the lab and takes it.   ....

    d Hank finds his wife.   ....

    e Sonny takes the lab.   ....

    f Ghost takes the lab.   ....

17 Answer these questions.

    a Why does The Wasp say "Oh, no!" when she sees the giant Ant-Man?

    b Why does the pod say "You can now leave the Quantum Realm?"

    c Why does Ghost throw Bill across the floor?

    d Why does Janet suddenly feel weaker?

    e Why do Scott, Hank, and Hope suddenly have to leave?

    f Why do Sonny and his men tell the police everything?

    g Why is Agent Woo very angry when the ant suit shrinks to ant size?

After you read

18 Read the last three lines of the story again. Discuss these questions.

    a What happens to Hope?
    b What will happen to Ant-Man? How does he feel?

19 Work with two other students. Take turns to be Student A.

    Student A: Find a picture in the book. Answer the other students' questions.
    Students B and C: Ask Student A questions:
    Who is in the picture? What is happening? What happened before this? What will happen next?

    Each student can be Student A.

Writing

20 Cassie is talking to her best friend about her dad, Scott. She tells her friend about his powers and his trip to Germany with Captain America. Write the conversation.

21 In a change to the story, on the last day of Scott's house arrest, Agent Woo gives Scott some of Uzman's truth serum. Agent Woo can ask Scott three questions. Write the questions. Then write Scott's answers.

22 You work for Sonny Burch but somebody gave you some truth serum. Write an email to Agent Woo. Tell him about Sonny and Agent Stoltz.

23 You are Janet. You are home after thirty years in the Quantum Realm. What is strange to you? What is the same? What do you like about today's world? What do you hate?

24 You have Ant-Man's or The Wasp's great powers. What can you do? When would you like to use your powers? When will they be a problem?

25 Think of a location from this story: maybe the lab, the woods, the Quantum Realm, the city streets, or the ocean. Write about it. What can you see? Write about the colors and the sounds. Use ideas from the story and your own ideas.

26 Do you like this story? Which part of it do you like best? Why?

27 You are Ant-Man at the end of the story. You are in the Quantum Realm, and Hope and Hank are not answering you on the radio. What will your life be like now? Can you get back? Write about your feelings.

Word List

agent (n) She's a Russian *agent* in the United States, so American *agent*s watch her all the time. She works for the Russian *agency,* the SVR.

ant (n) *Ants* have six legs. Some ants can also fly. They are very small but very strong.

arrest (n/v) The police caught the man and *arrested* him. He didn't go to prison, but he couldn't leave his home. He was *under house arrest* for a year.

atom (n) An *atom* is very, very small. You cannot see it. When something is *subatomic*, it is smaller than an atom.

control (n/v) The driver had an accident when he lost *control* of the car. The car was new, and he didn't understand the *controls*.

energy (n) Clean *energy* comes from wind, oceans, rivers, and the sun.

ghost (n) Abraham Lincoln died in 1865, but some people see his *ghost* in the White House today.

giant (n/adj) The tallest American was 2.72 meters tall. He was a *giant!*

laboratory, lab (n) The scientists tested their new idea in a *laboratory*.

location (n) "Please tell me your *location*," the policeman said to the caller. "We'll send help now."

missile (n) The missile hit a building, and the building fell to the ground.

part (n) The store sells *parts* for computers and cameras.

pod (n) She climbed into the small *pod* and flew up into the sky.

power (n/adj) She has a lot of *power* in the company; she is very *powerful*. She is smart and works fast, and she uses these *powers* well. She also *powers up* her computer at 7 A.M. and works fourteen-hour days.

prison (n) He went to *prison* for twenty years because he killed three people.

science (n) I want to be a doctor, so I study hard in *science* class at school. My mother is a *scientist*. She tests the water before people in our city drink it.

shrink (v) My new T-shirt *shrank* when I washed it. Now it is too small for me.

steal (v) He lost his job after he *stole* money from his boss.

suit (n) Tom wore his new, gray *suit* on the first day of his job at the bank.

technology, tech (n) I only change my computers and other *technology* when I really have to.

tracker (n) They put *trackers* on the birds and followed them on their computers. The birds flew from China over the Himalayas to India.

truth serum (n) After the men gave her a *truth serum*, she told them everything. She didn't want to talk, but she couldn't stop.

tunnel (n) It is about 19 kilometers from San Francisco to Oakland through the underwater *tunnel*.

van (n) I opened the door in the back of the *van* and put my boxes and bags inside. Then, I drove to my new apartment.

wasp (n) A *wasp* is black and yellow. It has six legs, and it can fly.